*How To Analyze People
With Dark Psychology*

*Blueprint To
Psychological Analysis,
Abnormal Behavior,
Body Language, Social
Cues & Seduction*

Table of Contents

Chapter 1: Dark Psychology, What Is It?

Introduction

Dark psychology is the study of a normally repressed condition in humans that causes them to prey on others. The condition is present in all humans, only that they exercise restraint and do not act on their malicious or predatory impulses. Humans that end up acting on these impulses are referred to as psychopaths. They irrationally harm or even kill other humans devoid of any remorse. Their behaviours are unmotivated, uncontrolled and unpredictable. Therefore, it is important to understand this condition, why it is present in humans and how to reduce the probability of becoming a victim. This chapter will go over the fundamentals of dark psychology and discuss why all humans have the restrained condition, why some act upon it and how the condition finally becomes unrepressed. It will cover the following topics:

- Understanding human behaviour
- The dark side in every human
- The Dark Singularity, dark factors and dark continuum
- Dark thoughts
- The deceptive personalities of psychopaths

Understanding human behaviour

In a novel called "The Road," McCarthy wrote a fiction story of about a post-apocalyptic world that had faced an unnamed calamity that wiped out most food resources causing characters in the story to become cannibals. The main takeaway from the novel was that, under the pressure to survive, all survival instincts kick in. These include hunting other humans for food. Under normal conditions where basic survival resources are available, humans restrain this condition. However, it is not uncommon for some to fail and act on their thoughts or feelings to exhibit predatory tendencies to other humans.

Dark psychology is focused on understanding the thoughts that can lead to this dangerous behaviour. In most cases, antisocial behaviours tend to be purposive and willful, therefore, be done with a certain end goal in sight. However, there are times where these behaviours are exhibited by individuals with no purpose or goal. Dark psychology concerns itself with such scenarios where humans are involuntarily triggered to exhibit these behaviours. Dark psychology experts maintain that the human psyche has an element that can trigger a person to commit atrocities without any intention. The experts also agree that this element is present in all humans and can cause just about anyone to become a psychopath. There are some factors that can accelerate one towards such a state and commit extremely cruel acts.

The dark side in every human

Dark psychology experts argue that all humans have a dark side. Steve Taylor, a psychology professor at Leeds Beckett University, explained that humanity has existed with a certain level of madness. Humans will, therefore, prey on others under certain conditions and history has already proven this. Before and after civilization, there has been constant warfare between groups and irregularities in the society have been the norm. Wealth and power have always belonged to a select few, violence has been rampant, minorities have been oppressed and there have been episodic colonisations and genocides. From the perspective of an alien observer, these are some of the happenings that could be used to define humans as savages.

The explanation behind all these cruelties is the dark element in all humans that is usually dormant but can get activated under the right circumstances. Most of these evils have happened on a wide scale and have been purposeful. For instance, armies fought in ancient times to colonize or push others away. Genocides happened just because one side thought that the other was more advantaged. Coups have occurred to topple dictators. In all these events, bloodshed, loss of life, torture and other inhumane acts have always been observed. However, there were tactful and rational thoughts behind these events. Dark psychology focuses on the commission of such acts without any goal in mind.

There is a capacity in every human to potentially cause harm to others without any explainable reason. In the news and dailies, there will be isolated reports of people that have hurt, maimed or killed others just for the sake of doing so. This behaviour is complex to define or explain and thus the reason why it is studied as dark psychology. Experts in this fields say it stems from the evolutionary predatory behavior.

Early man used to be a predator before learning how to make tools and venture into agriculture. Even then, predation never ceased. Since all humans share the same ancestors, they are all predisposed to preying. However, we do not go out killing each other because we have a lot of restraint and will not act on just any thought or feeling. This does not mean that we can stop these thoughts, we normally decide not to act on them. Most adults will have at one point in their lives had the feeling to commit cruel acts to others. For instance, a heartbroken man will get thoughts of hurting their former companion. Victims robbed at gunpoint, probably still feel like tracing the robbers and clobbering them to nothingness. If you were to be honest with yourself, you will see that you have also thought about harming another human. It is a wickedness that exists within us. This is completely normal as it is part of human nature. The difference between the normal human and a psychopath is that the normal human never acts upon the evil thoughts that cross their mind. This restraint is what separates mankind from predators.

The Dark Singularity, dark factors and dark continuum

According to the Adlerian theory, human behaviour is purposive at least 99% of the time. The 1% lies within a realm known as the dark singularity. This is where man's predation tendencies lie and actions taken within this realm have no purpose. Any thought that crosses one's mind within this realm is acted upon. If one's mind relapses to this singularity and a thought comes across their mind to set their neighbor's house on fire, they will do so without any second thoughts. All actions done are also devoid of remorse or compassion. To a psychopath, anyone and everyone is a potential victim. The victimization they dispense also knows no boundaries as they perceive that it is deserved. Any person that falls into the dark singularity is led to this by a dark factor.

A dark factor is a drive to prey or destroy others. A serial killer will be driven by the desire to kill other people just as an arsonist will have an irresistible urge to set buildings on fire. Forensic investigators, legal authorities and researchers have questioned many convicted psychopaths to understand how they fell into their dark paths. In many cases, the psychopaths would have a strong dark factor that quickly drove them into the dark singularity. If one had the dark factor of torching houses, after repeated arson incidences, they would have fallen into the inescapable dark singularity. The dark factor would keep exerting some pressure on the psychopath to victimize others by torching their houses. These acts of arson will be done without any motive such as revenge and quest for power and wealth. Whatever evil thought comes into the psychopath's mind is actualized without any rationalization. In normal people, the urges from the dark factor would be suppressed quite easily. When uncontrolled, the dark factor forces one into a psychological tunnel called a dark continuum.

The dark continuum is the path that ultimately leads one into the dark singularity. Psychologists define the continuum as a progressive severity of irrational malicious thoughts and actions. Since all humans have a dark side, they can rank somewhere in this continuum. However, the normal dark thoughts will rank very low and this will mean that they are too far back in the path to getting into the dark singularity and becoming psychopaths. People that have committed atrocious murders will rank higher in the dark continuum. The areas in their brain that are supposed to empathise with other people will show reduced activity. After each atrocious murder, these areas will reduce their influence on a person's decisions until *a point of no return is reached*. This will be at the point where they enter into the dark singularity and lose any form of guilt and conscience.

Dark thoughts

It would be easy to assume that humans are benevolent, kind and compassionate. Many would deny ever having dark thoughts lurking at the back of their minds. However, the fact is that part of the human mind is inherently dark and once it is allowed to manifest itself, it does. The dark side of humans is often denied and its presence is hidden. However, it is still observable. If you have had a chance to play open world games such as Grand Theft Auto (GTA), you would understand the hidden guilty pleasure of the human dark side. Such games are platforms that are used to allow players to commit malicious acts without real-world repercussions. With a rocket-propelled grenade, a player will insensitively and irrationally hit a helicopter and kill everyone in it. Automatic rifles, crude weapons, punches, and kicks will also be used against other characters in a similar manner. The dark and brutal thoughts a normal person has in such games are similar in nature but different in scale to what a psychopath would have in the real world. Essentially people vicariously get to live out their dormant psychopathic tendencies via console games.

These dark thoughts are shared across all humans due to evolution. The tenets of evolution were that the fittest animals would survive and procreate. Therefore, predation was essential as it ensured sustenance of life, protection of territory and it also gave the rightful conditions for procreation. Man eventually evolved to be the apex species and unfortunately, this meant that he is also the apex of brutality. Brute force had to be used to fight, hunt and kill. Today, a pride of lions will hunt down a buffalo to feed on. A herd of buffalos will also gang up against a solitary lion or young cubs with the intention of reducing the population of these predators. Most animals will display similar brutal and violent behaviors because some of these have kept them from being phased out during evolution.

Therefore, violence and brutality are already imprinted in most animals. However, man is the only creature that will prey with intents different from survival and procreation. Taking birds, for instance, it is unheard of that a psychotic bird has gone around destroying nests built by other birds without any purpose. There have also not been reports of psychotic buffalos killing other members of their herd with no intention. In humans, there are countless reports of psychopaths harming and killing others for no reason. The presence of unreasonable malicious and predatory behaviour in all humans is mostly unexplainable. This is what dark psychology tries to shed some light on.

The deceptive personalities of psychopaths

Most of the inferences that have been made before in this chapter about psychopaths have referred to significant cases such as murder and arson. However, psychopaths will still carry out smaller and non-violent crimes. Psychopaths can be enchanting. Chances are, a psychopath will not be easily distinguishable from a normal person by the way they look or talk. This allows the psychopath to manipulate unsuspecting people. Their true nature is only discovered when they end up defrauding or harming people. A psychopath is emotionally detached and will not feel anything after committing a crime.

A research done by the Vanderbilt University discovered that psychopaths have a hyper-reactive dopamine reward system. They will, therefore, keep seeking rewards without any boundaries in the methods of doing so. Therefore, a psychopath that feels satisfied after successfully defrauding a target will keep doing so to many people. Simply put, anything that gives a psychopath some satisfaction in terms of the release of dopamine will be done despite the risks involved.

The expected exaggerated dopamine response keeps them focused on any heinous task they decide to act upon. An arsonist will meticulously plan when and how to burn down a house. A serial killer will also carefully plan on the best ways to finish off a target. In the psychopath's brain, there will not be any reason such as vengeance to harm other people. It is only the end result of dopamine release that will give them satisfaction.

The progress made in dark psychology has thus far determined that human's dark sides are unpredictable. Some serial killers will never harm their families yet others will start by finishing off their family members. It is difficult to also figure out whether one is going to actualize any malicious thoughts. There have been cases where criminals are set free after a lengthy stay behind bars but end up in crime yet there are other cases where criminals lead better lives after incarceration. Similarly is not given that punishing psychopaths will help restore their lost sense of rationalization, guilt, and responsibility. Therefore, it is best to study how to protect ourselves from them. This will be the focus of this book.

Conclusion

This introductory chapter has delved into the fundamentals of dark psychology, a study of a condition evenly distributed in humans yet so rarely acted upon. This condition is characterized by irrational predatory thoughts or actions by humans against others without any reasonable motivation or goal. As revealed, all humans have a dark side and thus have predatory tendencies. A brief look at history shows just how brutal, oppressive and torturous humans can be to each other. However, these malicious acts that humans have done have been purposive. The dark side of humans is normally restrained but allowed to take over under certain conditions. In dark psychology, the focus is driven to the few humans that cannot contain their predatory instincts or thoughts and will willfully act upon them.

The chapter has explained the Adlerian theory which says that humans tend to act purposively, at least the normal ones. Conversely, psychopaths are not driven by any purpose or reasonable goal in their actions. There are three important aspects of dark psychology that have been discussed; the dark singularity, dark factor, and dark continuum. The dark singularity is a realm in a human brain where pristine evil exists. Humans are drawn towards this realm by dark factors. Dark factors are the irresistible urges to prey on other humans. These factors, once acted upon, move a human in the path towards the dark singularity. All humans can be ranked on this path with psychopaths on one extreme and normal humans on the other. Whenever one commits heinous crimes against others, their empathy and compassion are gradually lost and they move closer towards the singularity. After committing such crimes repeatedly, their empathy, guilt, and compassion are lost and they fall into the dark singularity.

Lastly, this chapter has looked at the deceptive personalities of psychopaths. They can be charming and manipulative. It is not easy to tell apart a psychopath from a normal person just by their appearance or speech. Psychopaths are also cunning and meticulous planners. Research has been highlighted in the last section of the chapter that came to a finding that psychopaths had exaggerated dopamine rewards once they committed their heinous acts. This is what makes them take all the risks necessary to achieve a certain goal. The chapter has ended by explaining the unpredictability of psychopaths. The best way to deal with them is to protect oneself against their manipulation to avoid becoming their victim.

Chapter 2: Dark Psychology vs. Normal Psychology

Introduction

The previous chapter gave an introduction to a relatively new area of study in psychology known as dark psychology. In-depth explanations were given about the exhibition of predatory instincts in humans due to a condition that is usually dormant in normal people. This chapter will build a stronger foundation of understanding about dark psychology by comparing it to normal psychology. These two are close yet are so distinct that they are studied separately and focus on different things. This chapter will explore, compare and contrast the two to help you differentiate between them. It will cover the following topics:

- What is normal psychology?
- What is dark psychology?
- Comparison between normal and dark psychology
    - Similarities
    - Differences

What is normal psychology?

Normal psychology, which is the bulk of psychology in general, is the scientific study of the mind and behavior of a normal person. It, therefore, focuses on thoughts and behaviors that are usual or common in the society. Normal psychology is multifaceted and has many subfields. Each of these concentrates on a specific aspect of the human mind or behavior. However, these subfields do not yet comprehensively cover everything about the human mind and behavior. This is because psychology itself is quite new as compared to other scientific fields of study. Therefore, most of the studies in psychology have concentrated on what can be regarded as commonplace. These include common disorders, emotional states, thinking patterns, and behaviors.

The limited reach of psychology is understandable as it has only been in the limelight for the past 150 years. Prior to that, psychology was treated as part of philosophy as it featured in the works of many ancient Greek philosophers such as Socrates, Plato, and Aristotle. The philosophers only talked about general topics surrounding the mind and behavior such as free will and memory. An example of these discussions is Plato's allegory of the cave which questioned the mind's perception of reality. Psychology only became categorized as a science in the 19th century. New contributions were made to it that proved that it was a scientific field.

William James and Wilhelm Wundt are the recognized fathers of modern psychology as they brought new perspectives to it. William James developed a psychological approach called functionalism in the 1800s to explain the human mind. According to him, the mind was constantly looking for experiences. Therefore, psychology was to be understood from the perspective of what caused certain mental processes. A few years later, Wundt came up with a different approach to psychology which was called structuralism. From this perspective, psychology could be studied through introspection. In his approach, study subjects would be asked what was going on in their minds while carrying out some tasks. This method, however, was a failure as it gave inconsistent results. Wundt, motivated by the failure of structuralism, opened a psychology lab in 1875 and this founded the way for modern psychology. He separated psychology from philosophy as he saw it as a science requiring observation, measurements, analysis, and explanations.

From Wundt's categorization of psychology as a science, it has been found to have a broad scope touching on pedagogy, perception, motivation, emotion, personality, mental disorders and much more. Modern psychology is heavily backed by theoretical explanation. Some psychologists will carry out studies of the brain while others will either focus on how the brain processes information, how evolution has affected the human brain (nature) or how culture and society (nurture) influences one's behavior or mental processes. As stated before, the study of psychology has majorly been on the usual behaviors, thoughts, instincts and perceptions. This has left a gap in terms of the study of unusual and unexpected behaviors, thoughts and instincts. This is the gap that is addressed by dark psychology.

What is dark psychology?

The previous chapter gave an in-depth explanation of what dark psychology is. Just to recap, dark psychology, as explained in the previous chapter, is the study of a dormant condition in humans that causes them to prey on others. It is noteworthy that, while most humans can repress this condition, some are unable thus exhibit predatory behaviors. Dark psychology follows a certain path called the dark continuum in which all humans can be placed. This path leads to the dark singularity which is a realm characterized by involuntary predatory behaviors. Normal humans move closer to the dark singularity every time they act on predatory thoughts. These predatory thoughts are referred to as dark factors.

Dark psychology is focused on several personalities that come up as a result of humans exhibiting predatory behaviors on others. Most commonly, the society refers to these people collectively as psychopaths. In chapter 1, a psychopath was defined as a person that acts on their predatory instincts leading to callous and insensitive actions such as killing other people or torching their houses.

Dark psychology encapsulates many undesirable behaviors such as needless aggression, opportunism, and impulsivity. By studying what brings about these behaviors, psychologists are able to determine just how much danger they pose to others and what can be done to protect others from them. A social psychology professor at the Arizona State University has created the following list of personality traits that are found in people exhibiting dark psychology tendencies:

- Narcissism – they might not be out to harm others physically but they will crave attention to any degree. They thus become annoying to others due to their behavior of wanting to get gratification and admiration from others continually.

- Machiavellians – they are master manipulators and will cheat others in a quest to get something valuable. Machiavellians are involved in white collar crime such as social engineering attacks. An example is Bernard Madoff that used his senior position at the NYSE to defraud investors of millions of dollars.
- Psychopaths – they tend to be malevolent, callous, impulsive, manipulative and grandiose. They are often willing to physically harm others in their thrills to satisfy their predatory instincts. They have no forethought of ensuing consequences and do not care about those that get hurt due to their actions. Psychopaths can be socially adept and this makes them dangerous since they can make good first impressions with their victims and proceed to harm them when least expected.
- Sadists – these are people that simply enjoy cruelty. Sadists tend to prefer occupations that put them in places of power where they can harm others without much room for legal recourse. Such occupations include the police force, military or even religious leadership positions such as priesthood!

Comparison between dark and normal psychology

Similarities

There are just a few similarities between the two. The main one is that they both fall under psychology as a whole. Psychology is broad and it encapsulates both dark and normal psychology. Therefore, dark psychology could not exist if normal psychology did not. If philosophy and psychology would not have been differentiated, chances are that there would not be any dedicated focus on dark psychology as a field of study. Dark psychology and normal psychology are also similar in their approaches to studying the human mind and behavior. This is because they are dependent on scientific study methods aimed at obtaining results that have a theoretical backing or explanation. Further than this, there are not many other similarities between the two.

Differences

There are stark differences between dark and normal psychology. While normal psychology is focused on the overall brain processes and individual behavior, dark psychology concentrates on specific abnormalities of the human brain that makes an individual prey on others. Therefore, normal psychology will focus on the typical members of society while dark psychology will focus on the few abnormal. In chapter 1, it was noted that 99% of humans act purposively and rationally while 1% act involuntarily and irrationally. Normal psychology will be concerned with the 99% of the population which follows the definition of a typical human. For instance, normal psychology will be interested in knowing why humans get depressed because it is common. However, normal psychology will not have detailed answers for abnormalities that make people serial killers and arsonists. This is the part in psychology that is left to dark psychology experts.

Dark psychology concentrates on a region of the human psyche that can cause them to act involuntarily like predators. It is an important part of psychology because this region is present in all humans but inactive in most. To further understand the narrow distinction between normal psychology and dark psychology, let us consider Sigmund Freud's breakdown of the human mind.

In the 1900s, Freud came up with a topographical model that could be used to explain how the mind was structured. His model was that of an iceberg as shown in the figure below:

- *Figure 1: An iceberg*

According to Freud, the tip of the iceberg is the conscious brain and it is the mental activity that we know about. Normal psychology will major on this as it consists of thoughts and perceptions that normal people experiences. A licensed psychotherapist will focus on the conscious brain to help a client to better their lives, improve their cognitive abilities and cope with challenges. Immediately beneath the water surface is the subconscious and it consists of things that people are actively unaware of but can retrieve them from the brain. Memories of people, places, and events among other things will be stored here. Normal psychology can still understand this part of the brain since all that is there can be retrieved back to conscious.

However, the bulk of the iceberg that lies deeper in the water is what Freud referred to as the unconscious. This is what holds things that we are unaware of and will possibly not become aware of. According to Freud, it is the unconscious that holds primitive wishes and impulses. However, these impulses are kept at bay by the subconscious and conscious. The unconscious affects human behavior, influences, and feelings. However, humans do not know what is stored in this part of the mind. Normal psychology studies some aspects of the unconscious through cognitive and social psychology. Discoveries made about this part of the brain have been used to understand and modify people's thoughts, perception, and behavior.

An exercise you can try to manipulate one's thoughts is by playing rock paper scissors with a friend but plant an idea in their unconsciousness. You can simply do this by symbolizing the rock, paper, and scissors with your own hands before each round. The last image that gets planted to their unconscious is the scissors thus it is highly likely they will play to beat the scissors. You will have altered their thoughts to think in a certain pattern even before the games starts. In a 2010 movie called Inception, Leonardo DiCaprio while acting as Dom Cobb states that once an idea has been planted in the unconscious, it is almost impossible to eradicate. It becomes a resilient parasite. This makes psychological sense since the unconscious heavily affects even the most casual decisions that you make daily.

However, Freud said that there are some dark desires that have to be locked in the unconscious through repression so that they can never manifest. Normal psychology does not focus on these desires but it is what dark psychology is heavily rooted on. This is where the predatory instincts such as irrational wishes, immoral urges and violent motives lie. Normal psychology will be concerned about the normal aspects of the unconscious but have a minimal understanding of irrational and involuntary desires that lie in this part of the brain. On the other hand, dark psychology will not have much focus on other parts of the unconscious except the ones that contribute to irrational and uncontrollable thoughts and behaviors. This is where the line is drawn between dark and normal psychology.

Conclusion

This chapter has further developed the understanding of dark psychology by comparing it to normal psychology. Normal psychology has been explained and the development of psychology as a field of study has been discussed from the ages of ancient philosophers to the current modern psychology. Dark psychology has also been briefly revisited as discussed in chapter 1. A comparison has then been made between dark and normal psychology. The few similarities between the two have been explained. The chapter has then focused on the differences between the two fields. Sigmund Freud's topographical model of the human mind has been extensively used to explain how the two fields differ in their respective focuses of the human brain. Therefore, this chapter has broadened the understanding of dark psychology by delimiting what it is focused on and how it compares to normal psychology.

Chapter 3: Subtle emotional manipulation (covert and overt)

Introduction

History shows that natural selection has always favored people that were able to manipulate their environment. Early man was able to survive in the jungle because he manipulated his environment and made tools for hunting, shelters to keep warm and safe from other animals and weapons to fight. However, manipulation did not end with early man and neither has it been limited to humans manipulating the earth to flourish as a species. Manipulation, as a predatory instinct, has subtly been extended to the modern world and is now being used by humans against other humans.

Manipulation of humans generally involves the exploitation of their sensory organs and behavioral traits. As previously mentioned, dark psychology experts have observed that it is hard to tell apart a psychopath, sociopath or narcissist just from their physical appearance. These categories of people that regularly prey on other humans are well knit within the society. They are our doctors, lawyers, police officers, parents and children among others. Manipulation is one of the cards up their sleeves and they will commonly use it to harm others or get things to go their way. Manipulation can be hard to spot depending on how a perpetrator executes it. It can be done covertly or overtly depending on the situation or the desired outcome. This chapter will discuss the following techniques used in covert and overt manipulation:

- Covert manipulation
    o Victimhood
    o Gaslighting
    o Overuse of facts and statistics
    o Time pressure - urgency
    o Silent treatment
    o Guilt trips
- Overt Manipulation
    o Expression of negative emotions
    o Deception
    o Punishment
    o Projection

Covert manipulation

Covert manipulation is the hardest to spot as it comes through seemingly well-meaning or harmless gestures at first. The manipulator uses these veiled attempts to make a victim unconsciously fall into their traps where they can easily control them. Chances are that the victims will not become aware of the fact that they are being controlled. They will feel as if their actions are out of their own volition while they are not. Covert manipulation techniques include the following:

Victimhood

The manipulator will prey on targets by playing victim to exaggerated issues of personal nature such as health complications, workplace issues or troubles in their relationships. This technique is used to quickly elicit sympathy from a target. Sympathy will lead then to the target agreeing to offer some help. Since the manipulator plays weak and powerless, the target's good will take over and they will feel obligated to help out the best they can. The manipulator will then have the golden chance to request for anything they want from the target.

Victimhood is understood in psychology as The Victim Triangle because there are three parties in it; the victim, rescuer, and persecutor. When one person takes a role in the triangle, you will inadvertently take another. In any case, the manipulator plays the victim, blames a persecutor and you are pushed to take the role of the rescuer. For instance, the manipulator may blame a terminal illness for his financial woes. You will be expected to fill in the role of the rescuer if he or she, later on, says that he has no money for rent or food. If well-orchestrated, you will feel compassionate and offer to help. However, this method is most effective in the short term since the rescuer soon realizes that all the assistance given has had no effect in alleviating the victim's circumstances.

Gaslighting

This is another covert psychological manipulation technique whereby a manipulator seeks to cause doubt in the memory, perception or sanity of a target. This technique is commonly used by sociopaths and narcissists since it is effective in the long-term and gives them more power to abuse their targets. The manipulator's goal is to ensure that a target will doubt themselves and have to second guess their choices and sanity. This will force the target to become dependent on their abuser as they will see themselves unfit to make their own decisions. For this level of manipulation to take place, the manipulator needs to be in control of the environment of the target. Therefore, it can easily be used in parenthood, slavery, marriages, religious cults, dictatorships, the military and prisons among other places or situations. The process of gaslighting involves the following:

i. *Withholding information from the target* – the less informed the target, the more susceptible they are to manipulation. The manipulator will take control of the information sources that their victim has access to. He can use creative ways to discourage victims from actively seeking information from other outlets. For instance, a cult member may be ordered by the cult leader not to watch TV or log onto social media as that would amount to tarnishing their brains. The cult leader, therefore, becomes the source of information for the cult members. This can easily work in dictatorships or prisons where access to external information can easily be limited. For instance, countries such as North Korea have a highly censored internet so that they cannot access websites that have contrary information to what they have been made to believe by the government. When the only source of information is the abuser, it is quite easy for victims to be manipulated into believing that only the abuser is right or knows what is right for them.

ii. *Twisting facts to suit the manipulator's narrative* – an abuser will be economical with information and only share what suits their narrative. They will also change facts to show that they have been right all along and the victim is wrong. The victim's perception will be attacked with these twisted facts from the manipulator. Any knowledge that the victim has and is contrary to what the manipulator says will also be targeted. Eventually, the victim will become dependent on the "truth" coming from the manipulator.

iii. *Controlling the target* – the manipulator will want to control the victim and their environment. To do this, the victim is first secluded from friends and family. These are the initial points of contact that can alter or question the victim's beliefs and behavior. When detached from other people, the manipulator will have sole control over the victim's thoughts and actions.

While gaslighting can be used against all genders, psychologists believe that it is usually more effective against women. This is because of the social construct that women are supposed to be submissive. It is thus easier for someone else to cause them to doubt their views, beliefs, and memories.

Overuse of facts and statistics

A quick way to exert mental dominance over someone else is by presenting yourself as someone who is highly knowledgeable. Some manipulators are fond of intellectual bullying to make them appear as experts in certain areas. They will, therefore, use alleged facts or statistics that a victim does not know of. According to Mike Alvin, a 21st-century psychology expert, you can delude people to believe anything you say if you present it well. Unfortunately, this is not true because that particular psychology expert does not exist and neither does this quote. As you have noticed, a typical reader or listener will simply take quotes from alleged sources as gospel truth. They will hardly examine whether what they have read or heard is true. Manipulators exploit this to peddle facts and statistics, some of which may not be true, just to get an intellectual advantage from their targets. A target that repeatedly hears a manipulator dishing out facts and figures will soon start thinking that it is because the manipulator is highly knowledgeable. Therefore, the manipulator will assume expert power over a target and make them a victim.

Once the manipulator is seen as an expert, he or she can push a secret agenda with less effort as the targets will readily accept it due to the manipulator's intellectual superiority. This technique is at times used by marketers that want to push for their products. By simply stating some facts, even if they are not accurate or do not concern their products, they gain an audience with the market and they can push their own messages. In psychology, manipulators will use their new found position high up the hierarchy of intellects to prey on their victims by soliciting favors.

Time pressure - urgency

The best way to get someone else to agree to something they would not normally is by not giving them time to think about it. Manipulators are experts at putting time pressure on targets to make decisions even before the targets are ready. This causes tension and with the little time left to ponder through a decision, one simply agrees to the aggressor's demands.

Yang, Goodie, Hall, and Wu conducted a study on how decision making is affected by time pressure. They argued that a decision maker's goal is to make optimal decisions but with the least cognitive strain. In their findings, it was clear that an increase in time pressure led to increased risk-taking during decision making. This was especially true for decisions that gave the decision makers positive gains. The takeaway from this study is that cranking up the time pressure on a decision to be made increases one's risk appetite. They will, therefore, make more risky decisions given that they do not know entirely what they are choosing or committing themselves to.

Manipulators know how to use urgency to get their targets to agree to certain terms even before they are familiar with the consequences involved. Later on, the targets become victims of the manipulator's predatory demands and they cannot help but comply since they already bound themselves into contracts.

Silent treatment

Silent treatment is an emotional manipulation technique. It is commonly used in relationships, especially in marriages where one of the parties is a manipulator. The manipulator will deliberately stop engaging in form of communication with the victim. The manipulator's intentions are to place doubt and uncertainties in the victim's mind. The victim of the silent treatment will greatly suffer as they start getting intense negative emotions. They get a feeling of being inadequate, worthless, distanced and alone. They can feel that the perpetrator is pointing a finger at them but indirectly. They cannot also figure out what they did wrong to be treated in such a way.

The victims feel obligated to do just about anything to re-establish communication. This gives the manipulator room to ask or demand certain favors. For instance, if the manipulator wants money, the victim will gladly offer money even in excess of what was requested. The manipulator will continue leeching the victim using the silent treatment method as long as there is something they want from the victim and will not take no for an answer.

Guilt trip

This is an emotional manipulation technique that involves the inducement of guilty feelings in a target. These guilty feelings can then be used to control the target's behavior and make them bend to the manipulator's will. Just as silent treatment, guilt trips are most common in relationships and can seem harmless to the target at first until they become devastating. This technique is commonly used in communication and the manipulator will try and include a few guilt inducers when talking or texting. People that use guilt trips are often blind to the damage that they cause. For instance, a mother telling her kids that she has had to slave twelve hours just to put food on the table as a form of discouragement any time she is asked to buy toys or pay for trips is not aware of the long term consequences of such statements. In the short term, they will discourage the kids from asking for money or other favors. However, these statements are slow poison and over time will result in emotional distancing or resentment. In marriages, manipulative spouses can use guilt trips to indirectly pressure their partners to grant them favors. By inducing some guilt in their statements, they will coerce them to say yes to any request they have.

Overt manipulation

Some manipulators are not discrete with their preying behaviors. They will therefore openly abuse victims just to get their own way. The following are the techniques that they use:

Expression of negative emotions

This is an aggressive manipulation technique that is aimed at intimidating the target. It can be done through the use of strong body language or raising of voice to clearly communicate that the manipulator demands immediate compliance with any request or command given. For instance, recruits to disciplined forces have to regularly deal with the yelling from their trainers. They are also not allowed to talk back unless asked to. Most commands will be yelled out and the recruits will hastily follow them. Outside the military, the same is used in families where children have abusive parents. Simple instructions such as telling a child to do some chores are given by the parent using a loud or intimidating voice. This type of manipulation is most effective when the target holds fewer powers than the manipulator. They aim at fostering fear and extreme discomfort so that their targets quickly give in.

Deception

Manipulators are accomplished liars who can distort the truth to their favor whenever they need to. They will lie to accomplish their agenda even when there are glaring facts that are the opposite of what they say. Manipulators are also notorious for denying what they said earlier. They can make promises just to get a certain favor from their targets but when the time comes for them to fulfill the promise, they deny ever making any pledges. Manipulators can even twist conversations they have had to make it feel like their targets are the ones on the wrong. These fact-twisting efforts are aimed at making a target feel bad for challenging the manipulator.

However, it is quite easy for the target to figure out that they are being deceived especially if they have access to facts or recordings of promises made by the manipulator. Deceit is commonly used as a bait and switch tactic where the manipulator offers something in exchange for a favor. The target grants the favor and waits for the manipulator to fulfill their end of the bargain only for them to lie their way out. Manipulators can also lie about their true identities to targets. The targets can then easily get swindled thinking that they are dealing with legitimate people. In the cybersecurity industry, there is a particular type of attack known as social engineering that has been successful against highly protected organizations. It entails cybercriminals using falsified identities and communicating directly with employees in an organization. They can then ask for money, login credentials, sensitive files, and other favors. There are several organizations that have been hacked or lost money to hackers in such types of attacks. Yahoo was attacked through social engineering in 2013 leading to the theft of account details of close to three billion users! This is enough proof that deception is a highly effective manipulation technique.

Punishment

Long-term abusive relationships are often as a result of manipulative punishments. The manipulator usually results to physically hurting a victim just to get their way. There have been several reports of sex abuse spanning over decades where the victims are physically harmed and threatened with further harm if they report to law enforcement agencies or the public about their afflictions. There have also been reports of abusive parenthood where parents have mistreated, beaten, burned or insulted their children for years. This manipulation technique is common where the manipulator holds to a great degree the control of the victim's movements and social interactions.

The physical and emotional scars that result from the punishments have the effect of making the victims feel frail and defenseless against their manipulators. At times, an unconventional relationship arises from this and the victim becomes attached to the manipulator. There was a news article in the New Yorker that detailed how girls that had been abducted in Nigeria by a terror group known as Boko Haram were rescued only to go back to the terrorists shortly afterward. A bond had been created between them and their captives who tortured, raped and murdered them for flimsy reasons such as not watching executions conducted by the group members. Despite their knowledge of this, they would rather risk their lives to go back to the forests and rejoin the terrorists due to the strange bond. Punishment is, therefore, a long-term manipulation technique and the more a victim is subjected to it, they will bond with their abuser.

Projection

Manipulators can create a toxic environment around themselves yet find a victim to blame for it. Psychopaths and narcissists use this a defense mechanism to shift any feeling of guilt or responsibility to others. They will paint their negative traits on other person or blame that person for their negative or even harmful behavior. The targets are likely to be compassionate and will accept the projections from the manipulator. Eventually, they will start believing that they are the problem, not the manipulators. Parents to criminals or terrorists often experience this where they blame themselves for the behaviors of their children. If the criminal steals and blames the parent for not raising him or her well, the parent will mostly accept the guilt. The parent will also feel responsible for all the criminal activities that their child has committed. This technique is usually emotional and the victims start bearing the mental and emotional burdens of the manipulator.

Conclusion

Manipulation was and has been a way of life for man. It is what has helped him to conquer and flourish in his environment. There are however a few people that use manipulation to prey on others. This chapter has discussed the two categories of the manipulation techniques that are commonly used; covert and overt. Covert manipulation is hard to spot and might be seemingly harmless to a target. Overt manipulation is outrightly visible and the manipulator directly preys on the target without concealing their intentions. The covert manipulation techniques discussed are victimhood, gas lighting, overuse of facts and statistics, time pressure, silent treatment and guilt trips. The overt manipulation techniques that have been discussed include the expression of negative emotions, deception, punishment, and projection. The end result of all these manipulation techniques is the preying of victims by the manipulators with varying degrees of effectiveness in the short and long term.

Chapter 4: The art of persuasion

Introduction

The most effective tool that a manipulator has is persuasion. In dark psychology, humans that exhibit predatory instincts seem to have well-developed persuasion skills. They use these skills to attract their targets and once they have earned their trust, they prey on them. Persuasion is often referred to as an art. It is a product of creativity and imagination which allows one to get other people to accept to granting favors. Persuasion makes it easy for people to be preyed on without them becoming aware of it. This chapter will look at the following persuasion techniques:

- Reciprocation
- Obligation
- Concession
- Scarcity
- Commitment and consistency
- Liking
- Social proof
- Framing

Reciprocation

There is a commonly used phrase that violence begets violence or hate begets hate. The underlying meaning of such phrases is that humans will always respond in kind. If they are shown violence, they will respond with violence. However, if shown kindness and favor, they will respond with more kindness and favor. The reciprocation process works as follows:

1.   You grant a favor
2.   The person granted feels indebted
3.   You request for a favor from the person
4.   The favor is granted

Reciprocation is used more often than one can tell. Since childhood, one is taught to respond to any act of kindness with a thank you to show gratitude. That is a form of reciprocation. During electioneering periods, politicians will try to appear charitable and concerned with the lives of citizens because they expect reciprocation in the form of votes. It has been observed that some pharmaceutical companies give free equipment or provide gifts to hospitals and this leads to doctors reciprocating by prescribing patients drugs from these companies.

Reciprocation is highly effective in gaining the compliance of a rational person. However, it only works when the target is given something that they find valuable. Once they have consumed it, the feeling of being indebted fills them. Small gestures such as holding the door to an elevator open for one to enter evoke a reciprocation of a small "thank you." Favors such as paying someone's bill at a café or bar will keep them indebted and they will be willing to reciprocate with a much bigger favor. When you need any assistance, they will probably offer to help when requested.

Manipulators take advantage of the overpowering rule of reciprocation in humans to entrap their targets. They pretend to care and will be ready to offer money, gifts or free services to be perceived as philanthropists. However, they will have planned ahead on how they will prey on people that have accepted their freebies or assistance. Manipulators can start a sequence of requesting favors from someone just because of the bait one took in the form of a free gift. This will go on until the feeling of being indebted goes away.

Reciprocation has proven to work even on a global scale. Superpower nations will often offer to give relief money and food or offer military support to weaker countries at no charge. However, the same nations will quickly flood the country they are supposedly assisting with cheap exports or will start taking away natural resources from it without much of a negotiation. Reciprocation is, therefore, highly effective at any scale and comes with high rates of success.

Obligation

There is a concept taught in law schools known as the duty to rescue. In countries where this tort law is observed, one can be held legally liable for not coming to the rescue of another person that could be injured or killed if not rescued. There are many obligations that all rational humans are supposed to honor. These include moral, contractual, legal or religious obligations. One group of people that experience the first-hand effects of contractual obligations are helpdesk officers who are charged with offering support to clients or other staff. They are regularly insulted and they cannot do anything except politely requesting callers to be patient as they offer the assistance as they are contractually obligated to. Manipulators take advantage of an individual's sense of obligation in a number of ways. They might present themselves as people in need of help.

There are carjacking incidences where the victims innocently stopped to help a stranded 'couple' on the side of the road that had a flat tire. Manipulators are experts at creating the conditions that will strongly evoke one's moral obligation to help. They can pretend to be needy, crippled or abandoned among other things just to get free money or other resources from unsuspecting people. The success of obligation as a form of persuasion depends on the nurturing of the target. People brought up in cultures where it is a must to assist those in need can easily become victims of manipulators that use obligation. The success rate of this method is, therefore, depended on the sense of obligation of the target.

Concession

Sometimes, the best way to win is to accept a small loss at first. There is a secret move used by debaters to disarm their opponents whereby they agree with the opponent only to finish off by hammering a strong point of disapproval. This move first dilutes the effect of a point made by an opponent and gives one the room to raise a stronger one. In persuasion, manipulators are always looking for ways to ease tense moments or any conflicts with their targets in order to settle for deals where they stand to benefit the most. In any deal, the two parties will be looking to further their interests thus it is expected that there will be tense moments. The manipulator only wants to take advantage of the target but has to ensure that they do not end up in serious conflicts which will spoil the chances of this happening. They, therefore, give the targets the first go in coming up with a deal only for the manipulator to agree to it but add other terms where they will benefit.

The manipulator will aim to give the target a sugar-coated deal or agreement with long-term ramifications. The target will be given room to make the initial offer or request and the manipulator will accept it. However, the manipulator will proceed to add some terms or make a request for another favor in return. By first agreeing to the demands of the target, the manipulator will have given himself or herself a platform to get what they really needed from the other party.

Recently, there have been concerns with the loan conditions a leading Asian country has been giving loans to others with unfavorable terms to get them into debt traps. For instance, the country agreed to give Sri Lanka a loan but also took over Sri Lanka's port for a period of 100 years. There were some terms in the loan agreement to facilitate for the port to be taken as collateral and the chicken came home to roost when Sri Lanka was unable to service the loan. Sri Lanka got the loan it requested but the aim of the loaner was to get control of a vital port in a trade route. Concession is also used to the advantage of employers during the hiring process. Some employers will agree to give the job applicant the salary they have requested but come up with borderline slavery contract terms. Concession is powerful if the other party is under pressure or has fewer powers. This allows them to easily be taken advantage of. This technique is quite effective but its success might vary with the manipulator's patience.

Scarcity

In business, prices of commodities follow the normal pattern where they are dictated by the demand and supply forces in a market. Scarcity, therefore, pushes the prices of commodities high. In persuasion, scarcity can be artificially created just to cause a target to take deals that are not good in the first place. Such deals will end up being used to prey on them by manipulators. A common trick that is used by marketers to persuade buyers when shopping are 1-day sales and limited offers. A buyer will, therefore, find it prudent to purchase an item on a 1-day sale because they might never get another chance to buy it with such an offer. Persuasion works in a similar way. The targets are meant to believe that they are about to miss something big. They will, therefore, act promptly motivated not to miss out.

Manipulators mostly introduce scarcity through urgency. If people are left to ponder a choice for a long duration, they will find out that it is not worthwhile or they will delay in making the choice. Manipulators do not want their targets to find out the scam in the deals they offer thus will always try to hurry up the decision making process. For instance, people that have been victims of pyramid schemes will have gotten themselves into get-rich-quick agreements after taking very little time to actually think about what they were agreeing too.

In 2017, there was a high craze for Bitcoin, a cryptocurrency that was sold as a promise to many that the money they invested in it would quickly grow. This craze increased led to a sharp increase in the price of the cryptocurrency coin. In August 2017, the price was at $4000 per coin but the surge in demand quickly brought the price to $19000 five months later. At this point, people were being told to hurry and buy Bitcoins even at such exaggerated prices as they would still keep gaining value. Unfortunately, the value of the coin quickly pummeled down to below $2000 later in 2018 leading to many people making huge losses. This might not be tied to manipulation, but it is a clear show of how the promise of quick rewards easily persuades people into short sighted investments that they are barely familiar with.

Scarcity has a high rate of success if the targets succumb to the high-pressure environment they are put in by the manipulators. The fear of missing out will cause the targets to irrationally agree to some deals and it is always too late before they realize that they have been scammed and are just being preyed on.

Commitment and consistency

Most people remain consistent with what they have already committed to. They are also likely to follow the same choices they made earlier if presented with the same options as before. This is because the human brain tries as much as possible to follow the path of least strain. Instead of having to reprocess data to come up with a choice, it simply reaffirms what it arrived at earlier. It has been proven that the simple act of asking people whether they would turn out to vote leads to a high follow-through rate for those that say they will vote. Since they are aware that they have already committed to voting, they will have to fulfill this by physically going to vote.

Manipulators can easily get people into commitments and they will easily take advantage of them when it comes to following through with consistency. In auctions, there is a common practice of two people trying to outbid each other up to a point they exceed the market value of what they are bidding for. Each of them has committed to getting the item being auctioned and will try to follow through with a higher bid to outbid the other bidder. People that have a gambling problem will usually spend up to their last coin in a quest to at least win something.

Consistency is usually based on previous experiences. For instance, addicted gamblers will have previous experiences of a successful outcome and will want to achieve the same in any round they play. There has been a scam going around that the FBI has branded as Business Email Compromise. This is where hackers spoof the email address of an executive employee and use it to issue orders to junior staff. Most of these orders include sharing of files or credentials and making urgent payments. Initially, the hackers might request for something of little value, for instance, the URL of a client's website. Once the junior staff have sent the reply, they will have made a small commitment to answering to the executive through the spoofed email. The hackers can then make bold requests such as funds transfer or credentials to sensitive computer systems. To the junior staff, it is more consistent to just give access credentials to their "executive" than to start asking why they need it?

The key to a successful manipulation through commitment and consistency is luring the targets with small commitments. With this small commitment, the target will be most welcoming to follow up requests that seem to be consistent with what they agreed to. Manipulators can use something as small as a greeting to start taking advantage. They can simply approach a target and ask "Hey, how are you?" If the target says they are doing well, the manipulator will simply say "Great, because I am not and I could use your help." In such a case, the manipulator will have gotten a listening ear since the target has said they are doing well. Through this simple response, they have put themselves at a level where they are socially obligated to help those that are not. The least they can do is to lend a listening ear as the manipulator starts detailing their problems and asking for help. They can then be asked to give generous contributions to assist the manipulator. For consistency, they will feel obligated to assist just to put an end to this commitment.

As can be seen, consistency and commitment are highly effective techniques for persuasion. A simple response to a greeting can even be used as a commitment trap. However, the technique has lower chances of succeeding in subsequent tries as the targets become alarmed after being taken advantage of. In some cases, however, the targets do not know that they are victims thus will continue falling for more commitments for a long time.

Liking

Most people will appreciate the feeling of being liked. They will also tend to like back those that like them. This is a commonly used tactic in marketing. Marketers will try to look smart and present themselves as likable people in the first interaction they have with a potential client. However, this should not be taken to mean that salespeople that do not fit the societal definition of beauty do not make sales. This is because liking as a persuasion tactic will be directed towards the potential customer. The marketers will try to make the customer feel validated and appreciated thus will be more willing to make a purchase. In manipulation, the same script is used.

Targets are usually made to believe that they are attractive, knowledgeable, thoughtful, careful or socially recognizable people among other things. Any form of validation can be used as long as it makes the target happy. This evokes the reverse liking process where the validated person will like back the manipulator or at least pretend to. However, there are some incidences where the targets do not value or care about being liked by others. Therefore, the manipulators have to seek validation themselves by trying to do something that the target likes. For instance, a manipulator could show up with an ancient piece of carving to an art enthusiast's home or office. That item will be of sentimental value to the artist and they will be impressed and immediately develop a liking for the manipulator. Once the manipulator has been liked by a target, taking advantage of them is easy. With the audience offered by the enchanted targets, the manipulators can make requests for some favors and chances are that they will be granted.

This persuasion technique is quite tasking. It is usually used on specific targets that are of value to the manipulator. The outcomes will vary depending on how effective the blindfold of validation lasts on the target. However, the effectiveness can be improved if the manipulator pleases the target even more. There are tactics such as positive reinforcements, gestures, and tone that can be used to sustain the bond between the manipulator and the target long enough for the mission to be accomplished.

Social proof

Animals will generally follow what can be referred to as herd behavior. Social proof is whereby an animal (person) assumes the behavior observed from other animals (people) in the same environment. A good example is whereby, we tend to laugh at jokes even if we do not find them funny just because other people are laughing. It is also likely that you will run if you observe many others running even if you do not know why. Herd behavior is deeply ingrained in animals and has helped them survive for years. The behavior portrayed by a collective number of people is thought of being correct. Even if it is wrong, the assumption is that there is strength in numbers.

Therefore, any decision you make is either consciously or unconsciously affected by what you have observed other people in the same situation do. The entertainment industry has already demonstrated the effectiveness of social proofing with shows that have canned laughter. Canned laughter is the sound of people laughing that is played in some scenes. The audience of the show will likely join in the canned laughter even if they do not find what is being shown to be so comical. If such an audience is, later on, asked how the show was, they will mostly say that it was full of funny scenes. However, all that was done was a psychological trick where they were put in an environment where everyone else was laughing thus they inferred that the most appropriate reaction was to laugh as well.

Social proof can be used as a means of persuasion by manipulators. All they have to do is convince you that everyone else is doing it. If they want you to get into a contract with them yet it is unclear to you, they can just show you the hundreds of other people that have signed the same contract. You will feel some assurance of security by the fact that many people have already signed the contract. Social proofing works mostly in environments where:
- There is uncertainty – the target should not know how to react. It is apparent that they should not have been through a similar situation from which they can infer. This makes it such that the easy way for the target to make a decision is by observing what other people have done before.
- There should be a uniform reaction by others – the target will be influenced by the herd behavior, not that of isolated people in the group. Therefore, the manipulator has to make sure that the other people in the same situation are making the same decisions. If the target sees some deviations in the reactions of others, they will also shift from the herd behavior and try to come up with their own decisions.

These two conditions do not need to be physically created. As seen in shows with canned laughter, which are mostly family TV shows, social proofing conditions can be created in studios. The manipulator can create them verbally by telling the target that many other people are making the decision they expect you to make and they have gotten positive rewards. The herd mentality will kick in and one will feel safer to act like everyone else or take the same decision as others. Social proofing is highly effective but only if the target is not certain or has not been in the same situation before.

Framing

A mental frame is a mindset that one has on a specific topic or person. It is the lens that will selectively collect and store information with the aim of guiding a person to a particular way of understanding things. In the art of persuasion, framing is a form of reality alteration where facts are purposively misrepresented. This is an age-old technique in which one becomes economical with the truth in order to achieve a certain result. For instance, politicians seeking re-election will often exaggerate the achievements they have made. Going to the election, voters will view the politician from the perspective of having a successful track record of service delivery. The opposition candidates are also likely to exaggerate on the failures made by those elected. This will put the voters in a mindset that everything is in disarray thus a new leader is needed and the opposition candidate is a perfect fit.

In marketing, framing is used to make items that have not been selling to get attention thus get bought. A crafty play with the prices is all it takes to do the trick. The vendors will increase the prices of the product for a short period of time which will be interpreted as a sign of scarcity or increased demand of the items. Afterward, they will lower the prices to the original price and say that they are 20% off. Buyers will view the product from the sense that it was expensive but currently the price has been reduced thus they should hurry to buy it.

Framing works where social engineers align reality and expectations of targets. Therefore, the technique only does half the trick and the target completes the rest in their own mind. There are ways through which framing can be done successfully. These are as follows:

1. Say things that create a certain frame – If a manipulator wants you to believe that he is a stockbroker, he will say things you expect brokers to say. For instance, he might receive a call and deliberately say aloud things such as "the most promising stock currently for day trading is X, I would advise you to forego Y for now. The market is currently bearish. I will get back to you about this later." With just a simple phone call and the mentioning of stock brokerage terms, they will have created a frame that aligns what you expect a stockbroker to know or say. If the real intention of the manipulator is to steal your money, they will easily do so since you believe that they are real stockbrokers.

2. Imply to a certain frame – if a manipulator is not so conversant with the expectations of a certain frame, they can just imply to it. They can simply put the targets in a mind puzzle. For instance, a manipulator selling counterfeit products could simply ask a potential target "do you know how many people are crying to us to supply them with these products?" The targets will imply that whatever is being sold is in high demand and they are lucky to have found the vendor.

3. Reinforce the frame – it is commonly said that a lie told many times becomes a truth. This is the same with framing. If a manipulator can feed to the frame, the target will have no doubt that it is true. If the seller of counterfeit products keeps getting many calls from "prospective buyers" when holding a conversation with the target, the target will be sure that what is being sold to them is scarce, in high demand and they should seize the opportunity to buy.

Framing is quite effective if the manipulator has good presentation skills. Once a frame is created in a target's brain, it will cloud their judgment more so to the desired effect of the manipulator.

Conclusion

This chapter has gone through the effective persuasion techniques that are used today. These include reciprocation where a target is granted a favor and the feeling of indebtedness causes them to return a much bigger favor. The second technique was obligation where a target is entrapped in moral, contractual, legal or religious obligations to help out. The third technique was concession where a manipulator accepts to certain requests from a target but adds other terms that only benefit him or her. The fourth was scarcity where manipulators artificially make some options seem to be scarce mainly through time pressure. This causes a target to make ill-formed decisions due to the sense of urgency but bind themselves in deals that do not benefit them.

Commitment and consistency was the fifth technique which is characterized by a target being trapped with a small commitment by a manipulator which only leads to bigger commitments that they have to honor to ensure consistency. The sixth technique was liking whereby targets are given some form of validation by a manipulator, thus become enchanted, and more willing to grant favors. Social proof was the seventh technique where targets are meant to take certain decisions because others have taken them. Lastly, the chapter looked at framing where manipulators create a certain mindset in the targets to make it easier to prey on them. These techniques are quite powerful ways to persuade people into making predetermined decisions or granting some favors. They have been used in the real world as the examples in the chapter have shown.

Chapter 5: The power found in the words you speak

Introduction

Controlling others is part of the human survival mechanism. Even when very little, babies can control their parents by crying. They cry to be fed when they are hungry, cry for affection when lonely, cry to be changed when they have soiled their diapers and so on. They are able to get what they want by simply crying. Later in life, it is obvious that crying becomes quite ineffective as a means of controlling others, thus one has to learn other ways they can use to gain what they want from others.

The most powerful way is through the selective use of words. Words can be used to create, destroy, give hope, stir doubt, and cause fear among other things. They can harm, heal, praise, confuse or humble people within seconds and without much physical effort. The words you speak can greatly influence your environment. They give you the authority to get others to grant your wishes or to comply with your requests. They can also cause you to despair, get into depression or allow yourself to be manipulated. Words are a double-edged sword thus have to be used carefully. Manipulators are well aware of how they can use words to their advantage.

However, if you also discover the power of your own words, you can become immune to manipulation and hold the power to control others instead of having them control you. This chapter will focus on how to use your words to control other people. It will look at:
- Basic principles of effective communication
- Priming people to control their decisions

Basic principles of effective communication

There are professions in which one has to know how to use words to their advantage. In law enforcement, suspects are questioned in a certain way to be cornered to admit, confess or give out information to officers. Journalists also have to know which words to use to elicit responses even when dealing with uncooperative respondents. In such professions, there are some basic principles that one has to know to exploit the full power of the words they speak. This section will look at these principles.

Listening

To use your words to bring out a certain effect, you have to know the context that you are in. The most important principle in weaponizing your words is listening. You have to be an active listener to interpret different situations or what others are saying.

Many debates end up in chaos because the participants do not listen to each other but rather are fixated on planning what they will say when their turn to speak comes. To correctly know how you will use your words to your advantage, you have to know how to listen and absorb what others are saying. You have to know the reasoning that others have before you can respond.

A common mistake that people make is that they try to stay in control of a conversation by saying more. In reality, you only need a single well-thought out sentence to steer a conversation your way. People like to talk and there is much you can learn about them based on what they say. They will even respond to your silence and continue feeding you with information that you can use to gain control over them.

Understanding the perspective of others

To be effective at communicating with people, you have to understand their view of certain topics. Failing to understand the perspective of an audience can lead to conflicts because you might say things out of ignorance. When speaking solely from your own perspective, you risk being misinterpreted by an audience. When using words to get something from others, you have to communicate in a way that they understand or see the world.

Making others feel special

There is a common saying that validation is man's silent killer. To further your interests in someone or to get them to give you something, you have to make them feel special. Once they are validated and come to feel that they matter, they feel at ease to share with you. Before interviews, media personnel will try to dig deep and find out any significant achievements that an interviewee has. When starting the interview, the interviewer will mention all these achievements to strategically make the interviewee feel special. They will become more delighted and more open to speak even about things they would normally hide. If you are trying to use your words to your advantage, you need all the information you can get to validate others. When one is validated, they will become an open book and cooperative, hence, you have a higher chance of getting what you want from them.

Being Self-aware

There is an invisible force that your body projects which is always felt by others. You stand a higher chance of taking charge of others if you strengthen this force. How you present yourself affects the impression that others get about you. Self-awareness is broadly scoped and ranges from how you look, walk, smile, greet others and even the tone you use when speaking. The human brain is capable of interpreting many things at a go. You might be giving an impressive speech, but no one will believe you just because of the tone you use. You might also be dressed poorly but speak in a convincing way such that the audience will believe you.

You, therefore, have to make sure that both your verbal and non-verbal communication play to your advantage. If you want to appear to others as the person in command, your tone, gestures, and facial expressions must portray that. There is a trick that some candidates use to help remain confident in interviews. They occupy as much physical space as possible by sitting upright with their arms wide out and then speak with a low tone. They are thus unconsciously interpreted by the interviewers as being highly confident.

There is another trick to avoid awkward collisions with people when walking in the streets where both of you end up moving left to right unintentionally to avoid bumping again into each other. All you have to do is keep your head up and stare at your destination. Chances are, if you look at people in the eyes, they will bump into you. However, they will give you the way if you just stare far-ahead. If people see that you are focused on a destination far ahead while walking, they will anticipate your path and move out of it to avoid such a collision. In the same way, it matters to be self-aware so as to control the impression that you leave on other people. People that hear you talk have to get a feeling that you are confident and have an end goal. They can therefore easily believe that what you are saying is purposeful and true.

These basic principles help others form a definition of you as you talk. The definition that other people have about you affects your chances of success if you want to gain something from them. If you present yourself as someone that matters, in authority and trustable, than you can control others.

Priming people to control their decisions

Your selection of words matters when trying to control people. There are some words you can use and get people's attention and even willingness to give you all you need from them. In many social setups, people will generally fall into two categories; leaders and followers. You have to use words that propel you to be the leader of the pack. Parents, teachers, managers, religious leaders, and politicians use words that assert their position as leaders or people in authority. These words impact the behavior and thought patterns of others.

If a teacher tells a student to never repeat a certain mistake, the student will likely avoid making that mistake even if they do not know what it can lead to. Similarly, politicians will tell people to vote for them or to support their political agendas and people will generally do that. They will avoid questioning these instructions because they came from someone in authority. The same can play in a group chat. If you are in a group chat and then use authoritative words, the others in the group will do what you tell them without question. Humans will follow those that show that they are in authority. Your goal should, therefore, be trying to assume the position of authority and then control others.

The best way to achieve these two is through the use of priming. This is where you expose your targets to something that will influence their subsequent actions or decisions. Priming happens unconsciously thus your targets are never aware of the end game that you are playing. Humans believe that their decisions are free and belong to them but, their decisions are highly affected by the subconscious. Therefore, anything planted in their subconscious will play role in how their conscious processes thoughts and decides. This gives you room to cause them to act the way you want or make them feel more willing to give you what you want. The following are a few examples of how you can prime people to increase their responsiveness and then control them:

i.   Priming people to be individualistic – if you want people to support a certain cause or feel empowered to conquer challenges, you need to make them individualistic. You can use words such as "I", "solely", "different" and "own" in your sentences to heighten their sense of self. This will make them more unlikely to conform to earlier views advanced to them by others and more likely to buy any individualistic ideas you have.

ii.   Priming people to be collaborative – if you need help with a task or want people to join hands, you can prime them before you ask for help or tell them to do something as a team. You can use words such as "work as a team", "stronger together", "us", "we will" and "our" in your sentences. Once they hear many of these words, their subconscious starts affecting their willingness to participate in a group undertaking or help out with tasks.

iii.   Priming people to be morally upright – in many cases, people taking public offices are supposed to publically take an oath of office. In courts, oaths are also administered to prevent people from lying. While talking to people and your goal is to make them confess or admit to doing something, you can prime their moral identities. You could begin with religious quotes or quotes from people known to have been brutally honest. Even though at a surface level they might not feel an impact, their subconscious is predisposed towards a certain moral identity and this will affect their decisions and behavior.

After priming people, you can then make your request and based on the thought you planted in their subconscious, they will most likely respond exactly how you wanted them to.

Conclusion

Words are powerful weapons that you can use to achieve any desired result you want in other people. In most cases, you can use them to control others. Controlling other people is a human survival mechanism and you begin showing it from a tender age. When you grow older, words become your primal way of controlling and getting what you want from other people. You can use words to evoke some feelings or cause other people to perceive you in a certain way. However, exploiting words does not mean talking more than others, it is all about being frugal with the words you use and how you use them wisely. As learned from professions that rely on the power of words, there are certain principles that you have to follow to control others. You have to be an active listener to learn more about your audience or targets. You then need to understand their perspective to avoid getting into unwanted conflicts due to misunderstandings.

You have to make your target also feel special and validated. Lastly, you need to be self-aware whenever you approach and start talking to others. These principles help others perceive you in the right way and this gives you room to control them. You can start controlling them by using selected words that penetrate deep into their unconscious minds. This is known as priming, where you expose people to certain things in order to affect their subsequent decision making. You can prime people to be cooperative, individualistic, morally upright and many other things. After priming them, you will have control of their decision-making process and you can easily get what you want from them.

Chapter 6: Vulnerability cues to look for

Introduction

In dark psychology, people that prey on others usually look for certain vulnerability cues to find the ideal victim. All humans are predisposed with certain characteristics that can make them vulnerable. However, these characteristics are molded depending on the environment one grows up in as part of the nurturing process. Therefore, the success rates of a manipulator vary with the nurturing of the target. The common human traits that work to the advantage of manipulators are; respect to authority, the desire to avoid trouble, guilt conscience, and the moral duty to help.

To varying degrees, these traits define one's personality. Many social setups institutionalize people by building their policies around these traits. Due to the exposure to different environments or experiences in life, some people gradually lose these traits. For instance, a psychopath no longer feels obligated to help others. However, these traits are never fully lost and with the right words or scenarios, they can still be exploited.

A hardened criminal will still care for his family just as a humanitarian aid worker will care for disaster victims. Even if the criminal will be ready to carry out atrocious acts against others, they still reserve small bits of the same traits that a humanitarian aid worker has. Therefore, manipulators have a working ground that they can potentially use to exploit anyone. Therefore, everyone is vulnerable but there are some that are more vulnerable than others. Manipulators only need to know which strings to pull in different people to start exploiting them. To determine which target can be easily manipulated, several vulnerability cues are used. This chapter will discuss these cues that expose the weaknesses of humans to their predators and how one can resist manipulation.

Vulnerability cues

Naivety

A good vulnerability cue that a target will be an easy victim is naivety. Naïve people often appear as lacking a good understanding of reality. They do not make choices based on their perceptions but rather based on ideals. For instance, they could have an assumption that their manipulators are simply friends or relatives that are in constant need for help instead of seeing clearly that they are just being taken advantage of. Naivety stems from empathy and the feeling of being obligated to help others. Manipulators can find out whether their targets are naïve by making early moves to test the levels of trust or patience their targets have with relatively new people.

Honest people

Toddlers are known for being excessively honest. However, as they grow up, they become aware that it is best not to share everything with just about anyone. However, since this is an outcome of one's nurturing, not all people get to learn this lesson. Some, therefore, remain to be too honest throughout their lives. Manipulators can easily take advantage of people that will only tell the truth about their decisions, suspicions, thought processes, personal lives and so on. A target that is an open book is a fortunate finding for a manipulator.

Materialistic people

One of the motivators for humans is to acquire more resources. They wake up and go to work to acquire sufficient resources that will allow them to lead comfortable lives. However, some people get too attached to the idea of owning as many resources as possible such that they become materialistic. Manipulators can cash in on this greed to pull such targets into questionable deals. The targets are usually given false assurances of exceptional material gains. Greed eventually plays its role and the materialistic people will be ready to part with what they have been requested for by the manipulators in order to get more wealth.

Elderliness

Unfortunately, the world is cruel and being old is a vulnerability cue. Many scams have been targeting the elderly because they are quite easier to convince. The elderly are already fatigued and due to physical limitations, they cannot multitask. If blasted with a lot of information that seems to be from a well-informed source, they will trust him or her. They are also less likely to discover a con. Therefore, they can quickly part with their money by giving it to people that offer to double it, give them and their families a lucrative vacation and much more.

The desire to please

There is a challenge most people face, saying no. Saying yes to requests seems to be the best option if one wants to make others happy, or to feel accepted, validated and in a happy relationship. Tony Blair once said that leadership is grounded on saying no, not yes. He added that it was often very easy to say yes. All humans share the trait of wanting to please others. They usually never want to enter into a conflict. They also try not to disappoint or hurt others. They would rather go out of their way than saying no and risk hurting others. Therefore, they end up saying yes to anything they are asked for. If the manipulator finds that the target has this desire to please, they can easily take advantage by making requests that imply they will be hurt if they are not granted. For instance, one could say that they are stuck in a remote town and have no money to live by then request for financial aid. The target, even if short of cash, will probably go out of his or her way to find something to send.

Low self-reliance

There are people who cannot rely on their ability to do things on their own. They must, therefore, have the support of others even when making trivial decisions. Low self-reliance manifests itself where people ask for advice on almost everything they want to do. For instance, they will not join a gym without asking someone whether it is worth it. They will also not purchase some items before someone else approves that the purchase is a worthy one. Manipulators will have an easy time preying on people that have low self-reliance. They will only have to bond or come close to such people and display their wide range of knowledge on many topics. Therefore, the targets will mostly start relying on them. The manipulators can use their new found position to prey on the targets.

Low self-reliance often makes the vulnerable people become emotionally depended on others. Their happiness, therefore, is rooted in other people's happiness. Their feelings are anchored on others. Emotionally dependent people are mostly lonely, an occurrence that is common when one is in a new setup. For instance, a new employee on their first day of work might show signs of emotional dependency since they feel all alone deep inside. A manipulator can take advantage and offer company and the target slowly becomes emotionally dependent. After a few months, the manipulator will be able to start leeching from the target. Even when it is clear they are being exploited, the victim will not complain since they are emotionally dependent on the manipulator and do not want to hurt them.

Pollyannish people

As mentioned in a previous chapter, it has been observed that some victims of abuse always go back to those that abused them. Defectors of countries such as North Korea have been seen journeying back to the country even though they were well aware of the negative consequences awaiting them. The problem is that humans try to rationalize everything that happens to them. They eventually find a way to make it right. They will even find reasons rationalizing why others have had to be hurtful to them. Manipulation thrives in relationships where targets try to justify why they have been manipulated and blame themselves for such.

Pollyannish people will also have an excessively optimistic feeling that things will go as planned, thus try not to focus on the negatives. They, therefore, always give the benefit of the doubt to others. Manipulators have an easy time with people that see only the positive side of things. They can be exploited without realizing. The manipulator only has to have sound explanations when questioned over some things. For instance, a manipulator could withdraw some amount of money from a target's account and when this is discovered, the manipulator could say that there was an urgent appeal from their family for money and that the money would be refunded. The victim will simply leave it at that and will assume that there were good enough reasons for money to be transferred without their consent.

Lack of assertiveness

Assertiveness refers to one's ability to express their feelings, opinions, and needs openly. However, there are people who will not express their feelings or opinions. Previously, there was a socially-accepted stereotype where women were associated with non-assertive behaviors. Though some countries still have this stereotype where women are expected to remain passive in the presence of men, most others of the world seem to have already dropped it. Non-assertiveness creates an ideal environment for a manipulator to take full advantage of a target.

Even though it commonly a result of stereotypes, non-assertiveness could also arise from low self-esteem and self-worth. Manipulators will capitalize on such feelings by making decisions that will go unopposed by the targets. In most cases, these decisions will benefit the manipulator and harm the victim. For instance, a manipulative boss could tell employees that instead of working 40 hours a week, they will be expected to work 48 hours. If the employees are non-assertive, they will not raise any complaints regardless of what their employment contract specified. The non-assertiveness will work to the advantage of the manipulator and the victim will remain timid and never express their opinions.

Making yourself a hard target for manipulators
The above cues are just a few that manipulators can use. Naturally, you will have some of the personality traits that are being actively exploited by manipulators. Many people only realize when it is already too late that they have been victims of manipulation. Therefore, it is of utmost importance that you learn how to move from being an easy target for manipulators to a hard one that cannot be taken advantage of quite easily. There are some basics you must understand about manipulation:

- Manipulation can be done by anyone and at any scenario – chances are, you will be manipulated by people you call family or friends. Manipulators do not have regards for relationship boundaries. Therefore, you should have at the back of your mind that anyone can manipulate you if they have such a desire. Finding out that you have been a victim of manipulation will most likely make you feel betrayed, taken advantage of and powerless. The manipulator, regardless if the type of relationship you have with them, will hardly feel a thing because they are only motivated by their own selfish desires. You should also be careful of strangers showing sudden care, affection or polite gestures that are uncalled for. Many manipulations begin with a phase known as a honeymoon phase to make you lose your guard and trust them.

- You can stop manipulation – You may not be able to change the person manipulating you but you can always change your personality to become immune to manipulation. You can only stop the manipulation if you avoid falling into traps set out by manipulators. You have to take charge of your decisions and not allow manipulative tactics to work against you. Only when you stop acting to please the manipulator will you seize control. Any relationship where you have to please others for it to continue is not worth pursuing.

- Manipulation grows – Manipulators are often trying to find ways they can use to gain complete control of you. However, they have to do this carefully to prevent arousing suspicion that may hinder them from long term gains. Therefore, you will most likely feel the manipulation setting in. It comes as a form of dependency or powerlessness against the manipulator. The more you tolerate the manipulator, the more you become weaker against them. Therefore, break the manipulation cycle early on.

Just to reiterate the above points, anyone can be a manipulator, you can stop manipulation and it only gets worse if you do not stop it. The best way to prevent against being preyed upon is by showing signs to manipulators that you are a hard target and then by not falling into any manipulation tricks. The following are some techniques that expert psychologists have recommended to resist being preyed on by manipulators:

- Take time – manipulators have to use urgency to create a scenario where you are forced to make important decisions without taking time to think about the options available. This is how people end up in unstable relationships, toxic workplaces, pyramid schemes and the rest. Always take time when making important decisions. You have to also make it clear that you do not need permission from the manipulator to take your time to ruminate about choices or not even make one at all.

- Do not justify your decisions – let your answers to manipulators be simple and straightforward. If you are coerced to join an investment group that seems to be a pyramid scheme, just say no and do not justify your response. By justifying a decision, you give manipulators a chance to try to convince you even more. Therefore, do not enter into an explanation or a follow-up discussion. This will discourage the manipulator from targeting you again.

- Tolerate uncomfortable feelings – manipulators often make use of uncomfortable feelings such as fear and guilt. However, you should be able to withstand exposure to some guilt or fear. If a manipulator tries to get you into a guilt trap, simply endure the guilt in the short term but do not give in to their demands. If they realize that you have a hard skin and their guilt trips are not working, they will stop targeting you.

- Call out the manipulation – as long as you there is a smooth relationship between you and the manipulator, the manipulation will continue. You, therefore, need to cause a disruption in the relationship and call out any manipulative requests or tendencies. By doing so, the manipulator knows that you are already on to him.

- Disrupt the manipulation – you have to state to the manipulator that you have already seen their end goals and recognized the manipulation tactic being used will be ineffective against you. Remember not to try to justify these observations so that they are unable to twist the narrative.

- Set your terms – if you are already in any form of relationship with a manipulator, you need to set boundaries early in advance. For instance, you could tell a potentially manipulative relative that you will not be able to grant any favors to them specifically. You will have placed a blockade that will demotivate the manipulator.

- Be ready to compromise after manipulation – you should be ready to turn the tables to your favor if you find out that you could be a victim of manipulation. You should be ready to compromise decisions or agreements you made with someone you have already proven to be manipulative. You can simply tell them that circumstances changed and you will no longer be able to do what you agreed earlier on.

Conclusion

This chapter has ventured into the core of manipulation and discussed the cues manipulators use to spot easy targets. It has shown that there are some human traits which everyone has that can be exploited by manipulators. They, however, are present in varying degrees in different people thus manipulators usually have to figure out the people that can be easily taken advantage of. The vulnerability cues that have been discussed include naivety, honesty, materialism, elderliness, desire to please, low self-reliance, optimism and lack of assertiveness. Manipulators will interact with different people to see whether they exhibit these cues. Those that show these cues are seen as soft targets. The chapter has then highlighted that it is possible to make oneself a hard target for manipulators. It has listed several techniques that one can use to resist manipulators and manipulative tendencies. Effectively, these techniques neutralize manipulation tactics and drive manipulators away.

Chapter 7: Case Studies

Introduction

Leonardo da Vinci said that only when you are alone do you belong entirely to yourself. He added that if you are accompanied by another person, you only own half of yourself. In the context of humans preying on others, the meaning of this statement is that you can be taken advantage of as long as you are not alone. Therefore, solitude might be the only guarantee that you will not be taken advantage of. The previous chapters have talked about the fine details about dark psychology to help you understand why and how humans prey on others. In this chapter, the discussion will give actual stories of humans exploiting others. Manipulation is so broad that this chapter cannot cover all the possible scenarios in which it happens. However, there will be several cases for each of the two categories of manipulation, covert and overt manipulation.

Covert manipulation examples

These types of predators are stealthy because they first appear as likeable people who are very charming. After earning one's trust, they slowly start showing their true selves. They are not always outspoken, thus they might appear introverted. However, they are selfish and arrogant in reality and have disdain for those around them. These will mostly be reserved in the initial encounters with targets because their intention is to play the "good person" card until the time is ripe to start exploitation. The following are a few actual cases for this type of manipulation.

Anna

She was the victim's friend and they were drawn close together because she presented herself as a philanthropist. She often discussed the charitable causes she was actively participating in and the non-profits she was working with such as UN agencies. Her victim did not realize that all this talk was just to give Anna a good persona. Deep down, Anna never cared about anyone. The victim describes how Anna had an entitled and exploitative mentality in any friendship she struck. She would expect to be granted favors but would not return a single one.

The victim later realized that Anna was showing disdain to most of her friends. It seemed that these friends were inferior and not worthy of her company. Even though she was not explicitly saying this, her tone, body language, and attitude sold her out. Her friend started distancing from her when she got drunk and she opened up that all she wanted was for people to admire her or worship her.

Anna was good at invalidating other's feelings and countering what others said just because she wanted to be the center of focus. Anna thought that if one of her friends made a sensible point or expressing feelings that would evoke strong emotions would steal the limelight from her. Therefore, she had to be manipulative and keep everyone's attention to herself. On the other hand, she portrayed herself to the public as compassionate and philanthropic.

Tom

Tom was an entrepreneur and was often regarded as a pillar of the community that he lived with. He was often talking about virtues and moral values with other people in social gatherings. He liked using himself as an example by saying that he was led by strong moral principles, worked very hard to be self-sufficient and took responsibility of guiding the community. Any conversation he would get into with others would be about personal values and he would portray himself as the moral compass. However, a closer look at his family would show otherwise. Tom was absent in their lives. He would rather spend time with "the community" than with his wife or children. He would justify this by saying that his children needed to become self-sufficient and that his own father was not around much when he was of the same age.

Tom would also talk about how hard his childhood was when his children asked for money just to avoid giving them any. He always knew what to say to shut down his own children when they requested him to be a father just for one second.

Besides his family, he became known for making promises that he would not keep. If confronted, he would simply ignore the confronters. For instance, he would make a promise to give a certain contribution to a family but later on fail to fulfill it. If asked why, he would just not respond. He thought that he was too good a person to be questioned when he failed to fulfill promises. He saw himself as superior to others and that is why he despised them so much when they tried to question him. This is what set him apart from regular people.

A normal person would apologize when wrong, try to be empathetic especially to their own children and offer an explanation after failing to honor a promise. Tom was hypocritical and was only interested in portraying to others a picture of an all-caring person worthy of being termed as the pillar of the community because it was good for his business. He wanted to be perceived as the perfect example of morals and personal values. He never wanted to take responsibility for anything. Despite his resulting financial success and elevated position in the community, his family generally struggled as he wanted to control all aspects of their lives. The children would never own toys or play the games their peers were playing. He was also beyond reproach such that no one in the whole community would try to correct him.

A covert narcissist mom

The victims, in this case, were the children in a dysfunctional family. They were robbed of their childhood and treated as emotional garbage bins by their own mother. At first, they thought that they were stuck in a family where the father was the predator and would abuse them physically, verbally and emotionally. However, they soon realized that their mother was not any much better. The mom used to dump all her problems on her children yet never listen to their own problems. The mom would occasionally spew all the problems to her daughter. However, when the daughter had problems of her own, her mom did not want to offer any assistance.

The mom watched for years as the overt narcissistic father abused the children and she did not even try to help. She would victim-blame the children at times and even side with the abusive father. However, when the father became abusive to her as well, she would cry to her children and they would have to comfort her. This was the equivalent of reverse parenting where the children were expected to play the role of being the parents. The mom would make it seem that it was the role of the child to take care of her as a mom whenever she was physically or verbally abused by the father. Even though the mom would not step in and help the children when they were verbally or physically abused by the father, she would exploit their emotional resources when she was the victim. The children therefore grew up in an unstable family with no parents to lean on.

Covert manipulators prefer being at the center of attention. They are low-key dictatorial and tyrannical. They will also keep telling others that they are good people with reputable traits. This is the technique they mostly use to lure more people into liking them just before they decide to start preying on them. Covert narcissists are only known by those close in their lives such as friends or family. They will conceal this to all others. However, they like to openly express how empathic, philanthropic or reputable they are and thus you can use all these as red flags for manipulation. Good people do not go around boasting of their goodness, their actions speak for themselves.

Covert manipulators also say cruel things in a calm way. Victims take a lot of time realizing the true identities of these people because of the cognitive dissonance. When someone is doing good deeds in public but cruel ones in private, a victim will not know how to interpret the cruel actions. They will even try to rationalize why the person is doing these deeds. However, after a lengthy observation, it will be clear that the narcissist has two faces, one is meant for the public eye while the cruel one is for private life.

Overt manipulation

In overt manipulation, the perpetrator does not hide the fact that they are preying on others. Overt manipulators have an imagined and unrealistic superior status that makes them see others as inferior. An overt narcissist has an exaggerated feeling of self-importance, brilliance, superiority, competitive and inflated ego. This causes them to want to dominate, exploit, devalue and have a condescending attitude towards others. They tend to show emotions such as excitement, boredom, anger, and jealousy. They have unpredictable temperaments, use a direct approach to targets, and take actions that are impulsive, risky and lacking conscientiousness. They are intensely competitive, aggressive and want to ascend up any hierarchy in the shortest time. The following are case studies of overt narcissists, most of who enjoyed positions of power.

Idi Amin

As has been portrayed in many movies, Idi Amin is regarded as one of the most brutal dictators and the worst the world has seen in the last 100 years. He overthrew the elected president in 1971 and started an 8-year regime in Uganda which saw more than 300,000 people massacred and many foreign entrepreneurs expelled from the country. Like many grandiose narcissists, Amin had an unrealistic feeling of self-importance thus he sought admiration from everyone. Before showing his negative personality, when he took over the government in 1971, he freed political prisoners and promised that he would give back the power to the people. This made most Ugandans love and support him.

However, he soon began his tirade of massacres and then he would demand people to show him admiration. He also wanted to maintain the loyalty of his soldiers thus he would reward them with shops vacated by the Asian owners he had expelled from the country. Idi Amin had an inflated ego and some of the available documentaries from the time show him telling interviewers that Ugandans love him and that he was very intelligent.

Amin, like any other overt narcissist, devalued others. He would order for the assassination of the people that he did not like alongside their families. He even ordered the killing of his wife. Another characteristic that defined Idi Amin is that he did not welcome any form of criticism. He used fear to control people and secret police to kill anyone he suspected to be criticizing him. He was extremely concerned when a rumor that was spread that a talking tortoise predicted his downfall such that he ordered for the change of his guards and rescheduling of his travels.

Lastly, Amin lacked empathy. Despite his realization that he was ruining the country's economy after the expulsion of foreign entrepreneurs, Amin decided to stay in power. However, his reign soon came to an end after a failed attack against a neighboring country where his army was defeated and rebels took over the country.

A Bully

In an adolescent treatment facility, a new character coach known as Dr. George Simon observed a young man continually flicking the ears of a boy that sat in front of him. It was clear that the boy was displeased by this and occasionally would turn back to request for the bully to stop. However, he just went on unperturbed by the fact that his actions were clearly discomforting others. When the Dr. Simon reported this to the facility's management, he was told that the bully simply had some underlying anger issues or was depressed thus he was negatively channeling his frustrations.

Dr. Simon decided to confront the boy and ask him why he had been bullying others. The bully simply said that it was fun to do so. Therefore, he did all this just for the thrill of it and did not care about the consequences that such actions had on other people. Dr. Simon says that the response was the biggest lesson he has ever had about predatory aggressors. They are psychopathic and do not care about others. Therefore, they will gratify themselves at the expense of others. This scenario can explain several other bullying interactions where people offer to sympathize both with the victim and the bully by assuming that there are underlying issues causing the bullying behavior. However, there are many cases where the bully is simply a predatory aggressor and is not dealing with a troubled past but rather having fun at the expense of others.

Robert Pickton

He was a farmer from British Columbia and is estimated to have killed over 50 people in cold blood, most of who were sex workers from Vancouver. Robert is said to have occasionally driven around Vancouver and lure commercial sex workers into his car. He would then offer them money and drugs if they agreed to accompany him back to his farm. Under the impression that they would get paid a lot more, most of the victims would quickly oblige and accompany Pickton. However, he is said to have brutally murdered them in his farm and dismembered their bodies. He would then feed them to his pigs. Investigators also found proof that Pickton was also selling human remains alongside pig parts such as intestines to a company that processed products such as soap and shampoo.

The Vancouver police were lost of words to explain how they handled the reports of so many missing women that were found to have been murdered by Pickton. Additionally, there were reports that some victims that managed to escape from Pickton's farm yet police officers did nothing after being informed that they had been abducted and stabbed by Pickton. It is believed that Pickton's financial status might have played a role in keeping him off jail after such disclosures from his victims. However, a testimony from a farm worker was enough to spark off investigations into Pickton's operations that led to his arrest, arraignment, and sentencing.

Russel Williams

Chilling tales are told of a former Colonel in the Canadian Forces who was a serial killer and murderer. He was handed down several sentences in 2010, including two life sentences. Williams confessed to break-ins, sexual assault, and first-degree murders. In court, he pleaded guilty to all the 88 charges that faced him. Even though he was apologetic when pleading guilty, the nature of his crimes shocked many as they were unheard of in Ontario. Russel began his antisocial behaviors with simple break-ins where he would steal the victims' undergarments but do no harm. He then advanced to sexual assault and murder where he would forcibly enter the victims' homes, rape and then murder them. In a bizarre conclusion, he would steal their underwear, take photos of their corpses and pleasure himself on their beds. He is also said to have followed up with the police reports for each of the crimes he committed and keep some of the documentation.

In one attack, Williams gained access into the house of a female corporal from his base station, beat her up and murdered her. He took pictures of the whole encounter. Lastly, he proceeded to steal her underwear which had become a sort of a signature move. His last attack was against a woman he kidnapped and took her to his cottage where he tortured her for a day and then killed her before dumping her body. He recorded a 4-hour video clip of this encounter in addition to the pictures that he had taken. This is the crime that got him caught since police officers started looking for distinctive tire tracks that were left near the victim's home.

The law caught up with Williams when the tire tracks matched those of the Pathfinder he was driving. He was taken in for questioning where he simply started confessing of his crimes. Past his sentencing, the Canadian Forces were disgraced by his actions and burned his uniform and his medals were scrapped. His Pathfinder was also destroyed and crushed. Even though a prosecution requested for the video clips and pictures that Williams took to be destroyed, the court said that these would have to be stored as they might be useful for his parole hearing.

As can be seen from the above, overt narcissists pose a big threat to people. One pattern that can be observed is that most overt narcissists enjoy some positions of power. Idi Amin was a self-declared president, Pickton was an affluent man and Williams was a Colonel in the military. These positions of power might have played a role in delaying the consequences of their actions but eventually, justice caught up with them.

Conclusion

The chapter has looked at case studies from the two categories of manipulation, covert and overt manipulation. The first three case studies captured real stories of covert manipulation. As can be seen, covert manipulation often starts with the perpetrators wearing masks to appear as a good person to others. After they have earned the trust of their targets, they reveal their hidden intentions and start exploiting them. The three cases provided about Anna, Tom, and the covert narcissist mom show that covert manipulators prefer to be the center of attention. They also like being perceived as good people. Only the people that are very close to them know their real identities. Covert manipulators will often exploit their targets for lengthy periods of times and at times, the victims will not even realize. They use cognitive dissonance to their advantage where they confuse victims with their figurative two faces, one which is cruel while the other is empathic and charitable.

The best way to avoid such manipulators is to look for the hidden signs in their communication such as tone, body language and exaggerated emphasis on their good personality traits.

The second category of manipulation is more direct and tends to be physical. The manipulators mostly enjoy some power over their targets which makes them hard to fight. They also do not have to hide their approach like covert manipulators. The discussed cases in this type of manipulation were Idi Amin, a bully, Robert Pickton, and Russel Williams. In each of the cases, the manipulators did not hold back their intentions, they just acted as they wished. Besides the bully, the others had powerful societal statuses which protected them from any negative consequences that their actions had initially. As was seen in the actions they carried out, overt manipulators are self-centered and do not care about the suffering they cause onto others. They are also brutal and will not hesitate to carry out all manner of obscenities on their victims.

Regardless of the type of manipulation, it is clear that a manipulator is never concerned about the target. Therefore, the best way to protect oneself against them is to avoid manipulation before it starts whenever possible, and as soon as you can identify it.

Chapter 8: Conclusion

This book has explored a repressed condition that all humans have that can cause them to prey on others. Many people are perfectly capable of restraining it but a few will tend to act on the impulses to harm or take advantage of others. Dark psychology tries to explain this condition and how it is expressed. There are three important aspects of dark psychology that the book has described; the dark singularity, dark factor, and dark continuum. The dark singularity is a realm in the brain where evil thoughts exist. Dark factors are the urges to commit evil acts that pull one to the dark singularity. The dark continuum is the path towards the dark singularity. Humans gradually move towards the dark singularity whenever they act on the dark factors, that is, urges to harm others.

People that already exhibit predatory behavior to others are commonly referred to as psychopaths or narcissists. However, it is not easy to tell apart these people from a normal person. This is because, they are normal in appearance, speech and are very cunning and meticulous in their plans. However, they have a hidden agenda of exploiting others and will eventually do so when the time is right.

The given has given a noteworthy distinction that dark psychology is comparable to but not the same as normal psychology. Normal psychology is the broad study of the human mind and behavior. It encapsulates several subfields but most of them tend to focus on what is regarded as commonplace in the society such as emotional disorders, depression, and abnormal thinking patterns and behaviors. However, dark psychology leans towards the repressed condition that causes humans to act as predators against each other. The scope of dark psychology is, therefore, limited to the abnormalities in the brain that cause humans to prey on others.

The book has covered the two types of predation that are common in the society; covert and overt manipulation. Covert manipulation is the subtle type of manipulation in which manipulators use veiled attempts to try and gain control over their targets. This type of predation is common in close relationships and often runs for lengthy periods before the victim realizing that they are being taken advantage of. Some of the covert manipulation techniques involve victimhood, gaslighting, time pressure, silent treatment and guilt trips. On the other hand, overt manipulation techniques are direct, aimed at instantaneous success and are used effectively against strangers and people in distant relationships. Some of these techniques include deception, punishment, and projection of guilt.

A central problem in dark psychology is that of getting people to do or agree to what they would not ordinarily want to. It is clear that no one would willingly want to be preyed upon. Therefore, manipulators require the art of persuasion so as to be effective against their targets. There are several proven persuasion techniques discussed in the book that can be used to gain control over others. These include reciprocation, obligation, concession, scarcity, commitment and consistency, liking, social proof, and framing. These techniques can cause targets to take uncalculated decisions and to the advantage of the manipulators.

One of the positive highlights of the book is that words are powerful and can be used to influence one's environment. Manipulators use words to take advantage of others. However, if one can master the power of their own words, they can become immune from manipulation and even be able to control others. To use words to one's advantage, one has to observe the principles of effective communication to ensure that what they say gets an audience. These principles include listening, understanding the perspective of the audience, validating other people and being self-aware. After observing these principals, one can take control of others by interfering with their decision-making process. This is usually achieved through priming where some ideas are planted in the subconscious of others. People can be primed to be collaborative, individualistic and honest among many other things that the book has covered. Priming is effective at making people take predetermined decisions and this could be used as a countermeasure for manipulation or a manipulation technique.

The book has covered the cues that manipulators look for to find the ideal victims. Unfortunately, nature and nurture predispose humans with some characteristics that can be used to exploit them. These characteristics include the guilt conscience, moral duty to help, desire to avoid trouble and respect to authority. These characteristics define one's personality and are often to institutionalize people. They can also be used to tell apart targets that are easy to manipulate. Manipulators are usually looking for some vulnerability cues in the personalities of their targets to determine the ones that can be weak targets. The vulnerability cues covered in the book include naivety, honesty, materialism, elderliness, desire to please, low self-reliance, Pollyannaism, and lack of assertiveness.

Several case studies have been given to show the negative effects of humans preying on others. While covert manipulators can wreck relationships and permanently destroy the lives of their victims, overt manipulators can have even more devastating effects such as mass killings. Therefore, dark psychology reveals an important aspect of humans, that they can be the cruelest animals. The facts about manipulation are that; anyone can be a manipulator, it grows with time and it can be stopped.

Since the book reveals that everyone has the characteristics that are targeted by both covert and overt manipulators, it is essential to learn how to protect oneself from manipulation. The book details some of the ways that expert psychologists have recommended that one can use to resist predation from other humans. These methods include taking time to beat urgency, giving resounding 'no' without any justification to such decisions, tolerating any uncomfortable feelings that one might be exposed to by manipulators, calling out and disrupting the manipulation and having the willingness to compromise any decisions made during manipulation. Once a manipulator finds out that the target is uncooperative or is too strong to cheat, they will eventually stop. However, if one is seen to be accommodative of any manipulation techniques, the manipulators will see him or her as a weak target and continue their exploitative techniques.

Remember you can always break free from manipulation, but you need to identify it first!

References

[1] D. Simon, "Why Narcissistic Bullies Really Taunt - Dr. George Simon", Dr. George Simon, 2017. [Online]. Available: https://www.drgeorgesimon.com/why-narcissistic-bullies-really-taunt/. [Accessed: 23- Mar- 2019].

[2] J. Blanco, "Russell Williams | Murderpedia, the encyclopedia of murderers", Murderpedia.org, 2010. [Online]. Available: http://murderpedia.org/male.W/w/williams-russell.htm. [Accessed: 23- Mar- 2019].

[3] C. Mudede, "Death Farm", The Stranger, 2003. [Online]. Available: https://www.thestranger.com/seattle/Content?oid=16079. [Accessed: 23- Mar- 2019].

[4] J. Jones, "Real life examples of the covert narcissist good person mask", YouTube, 2017. [Online]. Available: https://www.youtube.com/watch?v=zWHqNpTj0Ew. [Accessed: 23- Mar- 2019].

[5] Braiker, Harriet B. Who's Pulling Your Strings?: How to Break the Cycle of Manipulation and Regain Control of Your Life. New York: McGraw-Hill, 2004.

[6] Hadnagy C. Social engineering: The art of human hacking. John Wiley & Sons; 2010 Nov 29.

[7] Schacter DL, Church BA. Auditory priming: Implicit and explicit memory for words and voices. Journal of Experimental Psychology: Learning, Memory, and Cognition. 1992 Sep;18(5):915.

[8] Carr TH, McCauley C, Sperber RD, Parmelee CM. Words, pictures, and priming: on semantic activation, conscious identification, and the automaticity of information processing. Journal of Experimental Psychology: Human Perception and Performance. 1982 Dec;8(6):757.

[9] Conger JA. The necessary art of persuasion. Harvard Business Review. 1998 May 1;76:84-97.

[10] Cialdini, Robert B. Influence The Psychology of Persuasion. New York: Quill, 1999.

[11] Hadnagy, Christopher. Social Engineering: The Art of Human Hacking. Indianapolis, IN: Wiley, 2011.

[12] N. Perlroth, "All 3 Billion Yahoo Accounts Were Affected by 2013 Attack", Nytimes.com, 2019. [Online]. Available: https://www.nytimes.com/2017/10/03/technology/yahoo-hack-3-billion-users.html. [Accessed: 14- Feb- 2019].

[13] A. Nwaubani, "The Women Rescued from Boko Haram Who Are Returning to Their Captors", The New Yorker, 2019. [Online]. Available: https://www.newyorker.com/news/dispatch/the-women-rescued-from-boko-haram-who-are-returning-to-their-captors. [Accessed: 14- Feb- 2019].

[14] Young DL, Goodie AS, Hall DB, Wu E. Decision making under time pressure, modeled in a prospect theory framework. Organizational behavior and human decision processes. 2012 Jul 1;118(2):179-88.

[15] Bargh JA, Morsella E. The unconscious mind. Perspectives on psychological science. 2008 Jan; 3(1):73-9

[16] Ferguson AS. Plato's Simile of Light (continued). Part II. The Allegory of the Cave. The Classical Quarterly. 1922 Jan; 16(1):15-28.

[17] G. Boeree, "Wilhelm Wundt and William James", Webspace.ship.edu, 2019. [Online]. Available: http://webspace.ship.edu/cgboer/wundtjames.html. [Accessed: 05- Feb- 2019].

[18] M. Shuttleworth, "Psychology in the Middle Ages - Beyond Aristotle", Explorable.com, 2019. [Online]. Available: https://explorable.com/middle-age-psychology. [Accessed: 05- Feb- 2019].

[19] "Alfred Adler: Theory and Application | Adler Graduate School", Alfredadler.edu, 2019. [Online]. Available: https://alfredadler.edu/about/alfred-adler-theory-application. [Accessed: 25- Jan- 2019].

[20] Buckholtz JW, Treadway MT, Cowan RL, Woodward ND, Benning SD, Li R, Ansari MS, Baldwin RM, Schwartzman AN, Shelby ES, Smith CE. Mesolimbic dopamine reward system hypersensitivity in individuals with psychopathic traits. Nature neuroscience. 2010 Apr;13(4):419.

[21] S. Taylor, "Humania: The Madness of the Human Mind", Psychology Today, 2019. [Online]. Available: https://www.psychologytoday.com/us/blog/out-the-darkness/201205/humania-the-madness-the-human-mind. [Accessed: 25- Jan- 2019].
[22] C. McCarthy and T. Stechschulte, The road. Prince Frederick, Md.: Recorded Books, 2006.